Better RESEARCH,

Better DESIGN

*How to Align Teams
and Build a Human-Centric
Company Culture*

ERIN B. TAYLOR AND MELANIE T. UY

SPONSOR

UNIVERSITY OF AMSTERDAM

AI SSR MOVING MATTERS: PEOPLE, GOODS, POWER AND IDEAS

Finthropology

MEDIA PARTNERS

NAPA
National Association
for the Practice of Anthropology

AAN
EASA APPLIED
ANTHROPOLOGY
NETWORK

uxinsight

THE HUMAN SHOW

Response #ability

ACTIVE8 PLANET

AMERICAN ANTHROPOLOGICAL ASSOCIATION

Building Back Better with Anthropology

By Gillian Tett

A couple of decades ago, when I started my career as a journalist (for the *Financial Times*), I was wary of telling people that I had a doctorate in cultural anthropology. Why? The discipline had an image problem.

To non-anthropologists, the idea of studying culture seemed exotic and colorful. But it also seemed dusty, old-fashioned; anthropologists had a whiff of Indiana Jones about them, in the popular mind. The word did not command the respect of economics, history, or even psychology; or not in the circles that read the *Financial Times*.

Now, however, this is changing - a touch - and I believe that the post-pandemic world could create opportunities to make anthropology newly relevant and visible. One reason is that anthropologists have been quietly creeping into numerous different corners of the business, finance and policy making world in recent years, doing important and fascinating research. Another is that the Great Financial Crisis of 2008 underscored a point that anthropologists have long argued: the world of money is not just about numbers or abstract equations, but human incentives, motivations, unspoken assumptions, and identities, too.

Credit, after all, comes from the word *credere* in Latin, meaning "to believe"; when trust is lost, finance does not work - as we saw in 2008. And while economists and financiers often downplayed this human element in the past, there is now a rising interest in behavioural finance and cultural analysis. Indeed, in 2011 Alan Greenspan, the former Federal Reserve chairman, even stopped me at a conference and asked for recommendations for books on anthropology; that was a remarkable sign of a bigger zeitgeist shift, given that he once epitomized a profession that worshipped ecocnomic models.

The rise of Silicon Valley in the 21st century has also increased interest in anthropology. Even the most blinkered technologist can see that digital technology is changing human interactions and behavior in important ways. Most also know that the human context in which digital technology is created and applied is important too. Meanwhile, a string of scandals around social media and concerns about the development of artificial intelligence has also sparked interest in the societal context of computer science; or, if you like, how AI can benefit from another type of "AI" - anthropology intelligence.

Another accelerant, though, is the COVID-19 pandemic. For one thing, this has provided a wake up call around the need to incorporate behavioral science into policymaking. Tackling COVID-19 has demanded amazing feats of medical science. Computer science has been useful too. But what has become clear is that we cannot stop the disease just with medicine, but we need to know why and how people assess medical risk, comply with lockdowns (or not) and their attitudes to vaccines. Culture matters, which is where anthropologists can help.

> *After all, our globalized system leaves us all so tightly entwined today that we cannot afford to ignore or deride other people, even if they live on the other side of the world; instead we need the type of empathy and curiosity that anthropology can offer.*

The pandemic has also highlighted a wider lesson about the need to be curious about strangers—and different cultures—in an interconnected world. After all, our globalized system leaves us all so tightly entwined today that we cannot afford to ignore or deride other people, even if they live on the other side of the world; instead we need the type of empathy and curiosity that anthropology can offer. If only Western policymakers (and voters) had been more curious about what was happening on the other side of the world in early 2020. say, they might not have ignored the threat of COVID-19 for so long—and learnt lessons from places such as Asia more swiftly.

Last but not least, the COVID-19 pandemic has helped the cause of anthropology in another manner: It thrust millions of people into a state of culture shock, shaking up our long-established patterns of work and leisure. We cannot take our identities, social networks and physical space for granted in quite the same way as before. That is scary. But—as anthropologists know—culture shock can also be liberating and exciting; it forces us to see the world afresh and recognize that the cultural patterns we inherit from our surroundings are not necessarily as fixed or "natural" as we think. Simply walking into an office, starting a job, or surfing online is a newly novel experience—and one that anthropologists can shed light on.

Will business leaders, financiers, and policymakers listen to insights about culture? Not to the extent that anthropologists might hope, perhaps. That "Indiana Jones" image will not die quickly; most non-anthropologists are stunned to hear that anthropologists are as likely to be working in an Amazon warehouse as in the Amazon jungle. And many anthropologists remain wary of working with business since they dislike the power of big corporations or capitalist markets.

However, I know from my own career that anthropological insight is invaluable when it comes to making sense of money, commerce and power. Many business leaders, financiers and other professions could—and should—benefit from it too, particularly when it is combined with other disciplines. And the rise of the sustainability movement and cult of stakeholderism suggests that there is a growing willingness to rethink business ideas, pay attention to issues that used to be ignored—and take a wider lens. Therein lies an opportunity for anthropologists to take a place at the table, as we all try to build back better. I hope the discipline seizes it.

Gillian Tett
Editor-at-large, *Financial Times*
Author of *Anthro-Vision*

Better RESEARCH, Better DESIGN

TABLE OF CONTENTS

Executive Summary

This publication provides researchers and their colleagues with tools and ideas to improve not only how research is planned and applied but also to embed research into the culture of organizations. In this way value can be created at many levels, both for end-users and for the people who work to meet end-user needs.

Companies depend heavily on user research to understand what their customers want, respond to demand, and make profit. But researchers working in companies often struggle to get their insights taken up into product design and can feel marginalized working in interdisciplinary teams.

The tendency to undervalue or misunderstand user research causes problems beyond loss of potential profit or the experiences of users. It also has substantial impacts in the workplace, both with respect to the satisfaction of researchers themselves and how their teams function. This harms everyone: Researchers feel dissatisfied with their jobs, and their companies forego valuable research insights.

Why would companies fail to do adequate user research—even though they know that it is important? Why is there a gap between what companies think user researchers can do and what they say they can do? How does this affect the ways in which companies manage knowledge overall? And how do researchers and their colleagues attempt to navigate these issues?

To answer these questions, we analyzed researchers and the people who work with them (designers, product managers, marketers, developers, and so on). We conducted interviews, held two discussion sessions on the topic with attendees from Europe and the United States, and we also dug into previous research on the experiences of user researchers within companies.

We found that the failure to value user research and researchers is shaped by two main factors: 1) organizational culture, and 2) differences in how people understand what research is and what it can do. Taken together, these two factors result in a swathe of miscommunications, silo-making, defensive practices, and oversights that prevent user research from living up to its potential and adding value.

To overcome these issues we encourage companies to build a strong research culture, using four building blocks:

Building Block 1: Values & Beliefs

Most companies have explicit values, stated on their websites and in their reports. But within all companies there is a wide range of values and beliefs held by different kinds of personnel. All employees—researchers and others—bring presuppositions from previous employment experience and academic training. A common tendency is to only consider research that contributes directly to tangible outcomes as valid. This attitude tends to overlook the value of "discovery" or strategic research, which is seen as resource-hungry and having uncertain benefits. Another component of this building block involves questioning beliefs about what research involves and how it should be done. Yet another issue that can arise concerning values and beliefs is how employees view their customers. A culture of curiosity can help overcome these issues.

Building Block 2: Roles & Relationships

Interpersonal relationships are the cornerstone of any culture. Issues with interpersonal relationships tend to arise when people do not have clear roles and responsibilities or when there is a lack of trust that prevents negotiating. In relation to research specifically, we see issues arise particularly when people try to contribute to a project or task, but their contribution is met with resistance. A significant portion of successful collaboration involves identifying your own preferences and strengths in the research process so that you can build teams with distinctive roles and contributions. Strong teams and communities benefit from serendipitous interactions outside of job roles and a culture of sharing knowledge and advice. When individuals take the time to reflect on their interpersonal relationships and to clarify their strengths and complementary roles with one another, then they are well-placed to build strong teams and communities.

Building Block 3: Teamwork & Community

Strong interpersonal relationships pave the way for strong company communities and great teamwork. There are several barriers to building strong communities and teams. One major limitation is the silo mindset in which the term "research" becomes exclusionary rather than inclusive. We encourage companies to think of research as a companywide activity. Bringing non-researchers into the research process means that a greater diversity of creative minds can share their own insights into customers, brainstorm customer research, translate insights into design, and align teams to serve customers better. It also improves employee satisfaction, since people feel more productive and better connected.

Building Block 4: Language & Communication

Researchers spend a great deal of time evangelizing research within their company, including educating colleagues, finding ways to disseminate their insights, and campaigning for different types of research to be done. An important part of this effort is finding a shared language in which to communicate between people from different backgrounds. Design teams, marketing teams, and finance teams may have their own terminology or preferred topics but prefer and understand particular forms of communication: such as data (qualitative/quantitative), artifacts (e.g., journey maps, customer profiles), or wireframes for product design. Our interviewees have found many ways to improve communication across teams and their entire company, including sharing insights weekly by email, producing reports, running workshops, developing metrics to measure research progress, and using a range of covert tactics to improve communication.

Finally we provide advice on how to implement these building blocks within your company. We encourage you to not stop there, but to also make an effort to build a broader research community of practitioners and companies. A research culture doesn't have to stop at the company level: We can all benefit from sharing insights, tips, knowledge, and best practices.

An important part of this effort is finding a shared language in which to communicate between people from different backgrounds.

Introduction: Why Research Matters

It was 2009 and the end of a long year of very hard work. Kathleen's team were proud to launch their new product: software that could make sheet music accessible for people with impaired vision or with dyslexia. They had worked hard for 18 months thanks to a European Union grant totalling over a million euros and they were sure their innovation would be a success. But after so much work and money, the software was only used by a handful of people. Kathleen, as the project manager for the R&D component, realized they needed to find out why. Her team started doing user research to find out. It turned out that what the developers and project managers thought users would like was completely wrong. More experienced musicians had already developed their own ways to make sheet music available to them and for beginners it was too advanced. Based on these insights the team were able to make some changes, but could not recover completely. It was too late—they should have incorporated user insights from the beginning.

Fast forward to 2018. On the basis of her experience with the accessibility software, Kathleen decided to become a researcher herself, as it taught her how making assumptions about users can cause projects to fail fast. Now, she is Head of User Research for a media company. When she began this position the company wasn't doing user research: They were hung up on analytics. She sometimes struggled to get the company to see the value of user research—that is, until the General Data Protection Regulation (GDPR) was about to come into force in the European Union. This new regulation was a potential disaster for a media company whose revenue depended heavily on targeted advertising. Would users give consent to allow their data to be collected? Or would they refuse, meaning that the company's revenue would plummet? Suddenly Kathleen found that her company viewed her work as critically important. Her colleagues were clamouring for the insights she and her team were generating as they tested prototypes on users. And their hard work paid off; the company navigated the new GDPR rules successfully and retained both their customer base and their revenue.

■■■

The above demonstrates something that, by and large, has become commonplace knowledge: We can't assume that we know what users want. Just because we designed the product and know it intimately doesn't mean that actual users will like it. These days there are countless books, blog posts, and podcasts on this topic (see Resources for suggestions). Everyone is talking about customer-centricity and the need to get out there among real people.

And yet companies keep making the same mistakes (which is why there is a Museum of Failure!). There are many prominent stories about instances in which this has happened. Just think of Google Glass, for example, described by interviewee Jeff as "[a] solution in search of a problem that brought up serious privacy concerns and led to a PR fiasco." This can occur when companies don't do sufficient research and launch products that are inadequate, which may cause losses of millions of dollars. All of this happens because they haven't taken the time to figure out whether there really is a market for their product, and if so, what design elements and features will make it a success.

No company wants to lose millions of dollars because their product flopped. But such dramatic losses aren't the only examples of what can go wrong when research isn't given enough bandwidth. In fact, they aren't even the most common. There are many, more subtle ways that research and its cultures impact companies on a daily basis, and they are often invisible. It's easy to identify failure when a product flops, but what happens when a product never gets off the ground in the first place? How much potential do companies have that is never realised? How can we quantify success and failure when we can't see what might have been?

The tendency to undervalue or misunderstand user research also causes problems beyond loss of potential profit or the experiences of users. It also has substantial impacts in the workplace, both with respect to the satisfaction of researchers themselves and how their teams function. As we have observed through our involvement in user research communities, and as Kathleen's stories show, many user researchers feel that their work is undervalued or underutilized. They struggle to communicate with colleagues about what their research involves and how it adds value. Some people see research as slowing things down. Compared with quantitative research, user research may particularly be considered expendable. As Anna, a user researcher lead at a design and strategy consulting company, told us, "We are the first role to be removed from projects when budgets are slashed. Clients usually argue that they know their end-users, and we can use their internal people as the source of data. Alternatively, they ask us to use their existing research

as they already know what needs to be built/delivered." This harms everyone: Researchers feel dissatisfied with their jobs, and the companies forego valuable research insights.

Why is this the case? Why would companies fail to do adequate user research, knowing full well that it is important? Why is there a gap between what companies think user researchers can do and what they say they can do? How does this affect the ways in which companies manage knowledge overall? And how do researchers and their colleagues attempt to navigate these issues?

To answer these questions, we researched the researchers: in-house user researchers and the people who work with them (designers, product managers, technologists, and so on). We conducted interviews, held two discussion sessions on the topic with attendees from Europe and the United States, and we also reviewed prior research on the experiences of user researchers in companies.

We found that the failure to value user research and researchers is shaped by two main factors: 1) organizational culture, and 2) differences in how people understand what research is and what it can do. Taken together, these two factors result in a swathe of miscommunications, silo-making, defensive practices, and oversights that prevent user research from living up to its potential and adding value.

First, we explore what "research" means and how it contributes to knowledge creation and foresight. We broaden beyond user research to discuss all kinds of research and how they contribute to product development and strategic direction. Many of our findings are applicable not only to user researchers but to all different kinds of research and researchers within companies. Part of the issue is how these different kinds of research work together to create a meaningful working environment and value for the company. Thus, we situate user research within the broader organizational culture and practices. We explain what we mean by

The tendency to undervalue or misunderstand user research also causes problems beyond loss of potential profit or the experiences of users. It also has substantial impacts in the workplace.

There are many things companies can do to build a healthy research culture in which researchers are valued and their insights are incorporated into company practices.

a research culture and why it matters (hint: tooling alone can't solve all problems).

We then spend the bulk of this report discussing the experiences of user researchers and their colleagues. There are many things companies can do to counter these problems and build a healthy research culture in which researchers are valued and their insights are incorporated into company practices. Indeed, there is a growing industry of research operations to professionalize this process.[1] In particular, we draw attention to the many innovative ways user researchers attempt to teach their colleagues about what user research can do, implement a strong research culture, and improve communication and collaboration. We were surprised at how many different strategies our interviewees have invented—ranging from overt, such as running workshops to educate colleagues about research, or developing metrics to communicate what research has achieved over the course of a year, to covert, such as finding ways to get a seat in executive meetings or having political conversations around the water cooler.

User researchers invest a great deal of energy into evangelizing their research, which is not surprising, considering that it is integral to their work. But it does highlight just how much time user researchers spend on activities that are not directly research-related. It turns out that much of a researcher's job involves communication, workshopping, bridge-building, campaigning, and politicking. In the best case scenario user researchers have the full support of their company to do this, including at the executive level. But in most cases their colleagues are barely aware that this work is occuring. Moreover, the Covid-19 pandemic has compelled many people to work from home, so carrying out research and trying to build a research culture has become all the more difficult.[2]

This report provides researchers and their colleagues with tools and ideas to improve not only how research is planned and applied, but also to embed research into the culture of organizations. In this way value can be created at many levels, both for end-users and for the people who work to meet their needs.

---

[1] See Metzler, Brigette. 2020. Leveling Up Your Research and Research Operations: Strategies for Scale. 2020 EPIC Proceedings pp 203–217, ISSN 1559-8918, https://www.epicpeople.org/epic

[2] This issue was recently discussed in a panel at the EPIC conference called "Debugging Distributed Teamwork: New Research", https://www.epicpeople.org/debugging-distributed-teamwork-new-research/

Understanding (User) Research

There are many invisible icebergs that can hinder a company from moving forward, or worse, sink it completely. Not all of these can be linked back to research. But considering the importance of knowledge in keeping companies innovating and providing much-needed foresight, it's worth taking the time to consider how research and knowledge are related, how they produce foresight, and how they can impact a company's trajectory.

Most companies do some kind of research, but their approaches and capacities vary enormously. For smaller companies with fewer resources, research might mean occasionally having conversations with users and implementing their feedback to tweak product features. Large companies often have dedicated research teams, sometimes split over several departments and specializing in different areas, such as user research, analytics, and marketing.

All companies—large and small—have something in common: figuring out what problems to solve, what kinds of questions to ask, how to analyze this information, and then how to translate it into products and strategies. Companies also need to make decisions about how to go about this process, including methods used and researchers hired. Sometimes these decisions are made early in a company's life and will affect the research process for years to come. But often companies find a need to shift gears: they begin by doing a certain kind of research, but as they grow they discover they have new problems that require new questions and new approaches.

In order to remain adaptable it's important that companies understand the different kinds of research methods, tools, and professionals available—and how to best use them. Details won't be discussed here, since explaining the different types of research would take several books (or perhaps even a library). Rather, the focus is on what user research is, the ways in which user research can be applied, and why research isn't just something done by researchers but is, in fact, a company-wide activity.

What Is User Research, and What Can It Do?

Sometimes people ask, "what does the user want?" but they don't realize they need to do research to answer the question.

Broadly defined, user research is any kind of systematic investigation of how people (or perhaps animals) use and experience products and services. Such products and services include physical consumer goods (washing machines or clothing), digital services (mobile apps, cloud storage, news media), infrastructure (trains, electricity), and information services (accessed via paper, digital, or voice). Until relatively recently companies primarily used the word consumer rather than user.

The shift toward favoring the term use' is a result of the digitization of so many products and services. We tend to see technology as something we use rather than consume the way we would, say, a food item or a piece of clothing. The way we conceptualize and carry out research has changed accordingly.

Types of Research

There are many ways in which user research can be applied. These include:

1. **Generative research**, including basic research and discovery research, to understand the company's customers generally (e.g., their demographics, user archetypes, customer journeys, customer pain points)

2. **Solutions-centered research** to test prototypes and adjust product features, such as usability testing

3. **Strategic research** to shape the overall direction of the company, such as on competition

User research can be both qualitative and quantitative.[1] An example of qualitative research may be when a researcher conducts observations and interviews with a user to figure out what difficulties they run into when they try to use a new product or feature. An example of quantitative research is A/B testing, in which two groups of users are given slightly different versions of the same product to test which is the most popular or functional.

Either way, user research always attempts to see things from the perspective of the person's experience using a product or service. The primary way that user research differs from other kinds of research is that it puts the user at the center of investigation. In this it differs from data analytics, which focuses on data for a large population. It also differs from social science research, which focuses on people, because social scientists don't usually focus on people as 'users' of anything in particular (although there are exceptions).

One of the most common complaints we have heard from user researchers over the years is that their colleagues think that user research involves only basic research or solutions-centred research. There is little awareness that researchers can also set about discovering the unknown and putting their insights to work for the company overall.

Gunjan Singh, a Product Developer at International Baccalaureate, explained that research is very much valued in her company, as they have a research team that does extensive research to develop educational content for schools. However, there is little awareness of what user research is. Gunjan is not in the research team herself and said that when she began her job, the researchers were confused as to why she was doing research at all, since they were already doing it. She had to explain to them that her research was vastly different to theirs. Whereas they were creating content, she was focusing on how users interacted with the platform and content, including the platform's interface and how the content was presented (e.g., length, appearance). Even when a company values research, it doesn't mean it understands all kinds of research.

Despite what their job descriptions say or what their colleagues think, user researchers work hard to find ways to do what they think needs to be done for users to be satisfied and for their company to be successful. Several of our interviewees described that when they started a new job they found that little to no basic research had been done and that product development was being prioritized, so they had to start there. Once this basic research is established they could then move on to more complex or exploratory research.

Other interviewees told us how they "cheat" to get valuable research done. An interviewee who works as a product owner in the education sector told us that when a department assigns her a user research project she will add on extra questions that were not requested, but will enable her to gain a more holistic and in-depth picture of users.

Another interviewee, who is a user researcher in the finance sector, told us that they do strategic research all the time, even though it is not expected of them. He said that when he began his job, his company had no idea who comprised their main customers. In fact, they assumed their customers were middle-in-

---

1 For more on how qualitative and quantitative methods work together, see Arora, Millie P., Mikkel Krenchel, Jacob Mcauliffe and Poornima Ramaswamy. 2018. Contextual Analytics: Towards a Practical Integration of Human and Data Science Approaches in the Development of Algorithms 2018 EPIC Proceedings, ISSN 1559-8918, https://www.epicpeople.org/intelligences

come people when in fact they were mostly lower in-come. Without that basic understanding of customers, they were heading in the wrong strategic direction and losing market share. The company's ways of working were not established to produce the knowledge neces-sary, let alone action it. As he put it:

It's exciting but it's also terrifying that nobody in the company has really been thinking about that or hadn't been communicating that to the rest of the team. A lot of our roadmap is defined by half-hour brainstorm sessions, which is scary. And often, again, uninformed by research. That's part of the current design culture that I'd like to see remedied, at least have a research brief on this thing that we're going to brainstorm today, give some kind of con-text rather than just pulling people and things out that they'd seen in another app or in their hobby horse.

As we will explain later, researchers have invented many ways to not only do critical research, but also to disseminate their insights throughout their company, especially to design teams and executives. After all, what matters to a company most is how these insights are actioned: what happens after formal research is completed. Insights need to be implemented if they are to be of use. Successful implementation of research insights is dependent on things being done right along the whole research trajectory, from identifying the problem to doing research and translating it into action.

Sometimes this dissemination process is easy because they work in companies where research is clearly integrated into a company's overall strate-gic direction.[2] But in the absence of a clear strategic direction, researchers—and the companies in which they work—struggle. We argue that research needs to be rethought. Rather than being seen as something re-searchers do, it needs to be viewed as a company-wide activity.

Research as a Company-Wide Activity

If you do an Internet search for "What is research?" you will find that most responses explain that research is a systematic activity that is undertaken to increase knowl-edge. This implies that research is carefully planned and considered, in line with the scientific method. And it goes without saying that people assume that research is something that researchers do.

In reality, however, the process of knowledge-cre-ation within companies is less linear and more dy-namic than this. Research teams certainly implement specific research projects with clear objectives that meet the common definition of research. But as we have already seen, researchers do far more than just research.

Moreover, it isn't only researchers who contribute to doing research and building knowledge. Research-ers usually work in mixed teams that include design-ers, product managers, developers, and marketers. Many of these people contribute to research in some way, even if it is not explicitly their job. For example, customer service staff learn about customers directly through having conversations with them. Developers working in companies that do no user research may take it upon themselves to talk with customers so they can improve features.

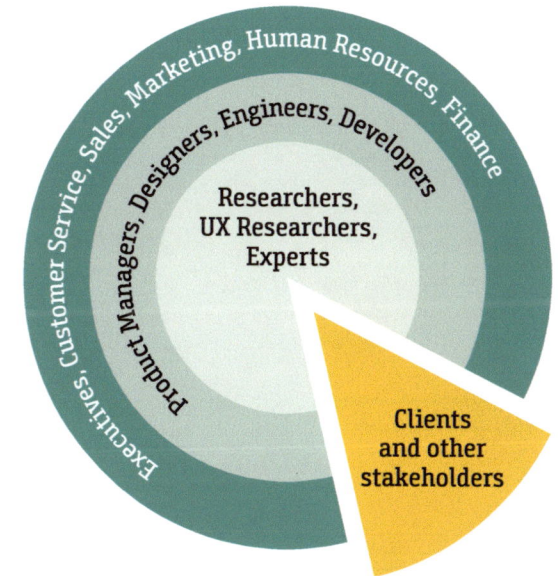

A research team can include a much broader range of team members than just researchers. All kinds of professionals in your organization and your client's organization can be involved in research.

2 For an interesting discussion of what strategy is, see Hoy, Tom and Tom Rowley. 2016. Strategy as an Unfolding Network of Associations. 2016 Ethnographic Praxis in Industry Conference Proceedings, p.427-443.

The process of turning research into action is a company-wide activity.[3] Or, at least, it should be, since the only way to scale knowledge is to bridge the gaps between different roles and teams. As Corina Enache phrased it:

> [t]ake people on the journey about research in your company more broadly, don't just share the results of the research because that doesn't take people through the process of sense-making. Better to engage people in the process of research.

In reality this isn't always the case. One of our interviewees, who works in marketing, lamented that her department usually has little idea what research the company is doing: they are "left out entirely." As a result, the marketing campaigns and metrics are misaligned with what their customers are actually doing.

Sometimes non-research colleagues need to be coaxed to join in the process. Kathleen, whose story we told at the beginning of this report, told us about how when she began a new job the designers on her team were very happy: "Great!" they said, "now we have someone to do user research!" She duly informed them that, no, she would be teaching them how to do research. They were surprised, but she was happy to report that they adapted quickly and became enthusiastic user-researchers. In her view, since designers are so influential on the user experience they should be involved in at least some basic research so they can gain direct insight into the effects of their designs.

Executives and high-level managers are also not exempt from user research. Research and design agencies are increasingly asking their clients to accompany them on fieldwork to see what their customers are doing and talk with them directly. For example, Joshua Dresner of Claro Partners explains in a case study that taking key project stakeholders on fieldwork can be valuable because it increases their empathy with their staff and customers, and it motivates them to take action.[4]

---

3 For an interesting case of collaborating to gain competitive advantage, see Tambo Jensen, Rina. 2018. Revitalising Openness at Mozilla: A Mixed Method Research Approach. 2018 EPIC Proceedings, ISSN 1559-8918, https://www.epicpeople.org/intelligences

4 Dresner, Joshua. 2016. Engineering Ethnographic Encounters to Lead to Better Project Results. 2016 Ethnographic Praxis in Industry Conference Proceedings, p. 415–426, ISSN 1559-8918, https://www.epicpeople.org

A Question of Culture

How can we ensure that knowledge is acquired across a company so that it can be put to use? As we quickly learned during this research, solutions have very little to do with tooling or protocols. While it is certainly useful to have platforms to share data and insights, or policy on who should talk with whom, in reality such formal solutions don't work unless a company has a healthy research culture overall. Moreover, even a strong company strategy won't be ultimately successful if a healthy culture is not in place. As one of our interviewees argued:

> Because, like, culture eats strategy for breakfast, right? You can create a strategy but if there's no culture where people are open to seeing the benefits or to new things then it's not going anywhere.

This claim is in line with a large body of research on organizational culture, which shows just how much culture impacts the workplace. A company's values, beliefs, habits, processes, rituals and communication patterns all have a substantial impact on employee satisfaction and wellbeing, and ultimately on the company's success.[5]

But no company has just one single culture. Instead, there are many different subcultures, sometimes aligned with departments or teams, or perhaps with kinds of employees based on skills, job role, level of seniority, or personal background. For example, people in entry-level positions may have their own cultural patterns, such as going out for drinks together at the end of the week. People with similar personal backgrounds may feel an affinity with each other and find it easier to communicate than with other colleagues. Teams that work closely together often form their own subcultures, with their own ways of relating and communicating, and this can help them to work better together (although, as we shall see, it can also create silos between them and other teams).

What, then, is a research culture? Simply put, it is a shared way of approaching research: It includes people's beliefs about the values of research, how it should be done, preferences for methods, habits and working processes, and especially ways of communicating about research.

There probably isn't a company that doesn't have a research culture of some kind. At one end, companies may be very explicit about the role of research in their organization and have strong practices in place to nurture it. At the other end, a company may not consider that it does research at all and puts little thought into it—but we find that even in these companies there is some kind of common understanding about the value of research and processes to collect information.

In terms of everyday or grassroots culture, much of it is generated by the researchers themselves and those who work closely with them. That is to say, much of it is a bottom-up process. Sometimes if a company has strong preferences with respect to research (say, ex-

---

5   Batteau, Allen W. and Gladis Cecilia Villegas. 2016. Cultural Change Management in Organizations from Competing Perspectives. 2016 Ethnographic Praxis in Industry Conference Proceedings, pp. 16–35; see also Dorland, Annemarie. 2017. The View From The Studio: Design Ethnography and Organizational Cultures. 2017 Ethnographic Praxis in Industry Conference Proceedings, p.232-246.

plicitly valuing evidence-based research or analytics), then the company's research culture may need to fit into constraints that travel from the top down. But it is certain that researchers and their teams will nonetheless develop many elements of the company's research culture, since they are the ones who practice it on a day-to-day basis.

What does a healthy research culture look like? Ideally there will be a strong synergy between these bottom-up and top-down elements. There will be alignment between all levels in the company as to how research is valued and put to work. Moreover, in a strong research culture people know how to collaborate to build insights, and products, together. And it is essential for a company to have a "culture of curiosity."

As Corina Enache, Lead of Organizational Development at Transavia, explained to us:

> The most important thing in fostering a research culture is that people have curiosity: not just the researchers but also other people in the organisation—curiosity is what leads to commissioning or doing research.

> Not everyone needs to be fully versed in research types and methods, but if people know how to ask questions then they will be open to new information and insights, which helps enormously in both doing new research and being open to fixing problems that arise.

Building a Research Culture

Building a research culture isn't easy. It relies on non-researchers across the company having a working knowledge of how research is done and what it can provide. It requires a shift in mindset to put the user front and center rather than the product or service. Companies may not know what research they currently do across all of their departments, and they may have little idea how to plan out long-term research or tie it into their organizational and risk strategies. And sharing research data and results requires solving practical problems, such as data management.

In this section we lay out four building blocks that are integral to creating a healthy research culture that benefits employees, the company, clients, and customers. For each building block we present the problems it solves and the solutions our research participants (and others) have found to implement it.

Building Block 1: Values and Beliefs

Most companies have explicit values, typically stated on their websites and in their reports. But within all companies there is a wide range of values and beliefs held by different kinds of personnel. These may relate to what the company's purpose is, beliefs about the

Building Blocks of a Research Culture

BUILDING BLOCK 1:

Values & Beliefs

The foundation requires a mindset shift from the definition of research, including auditing limiting beliefs.

BUILDING BLOCK 2:

Roles & Relationships

The second block requires strong interpersonal relations built on trust, boundaries, & serendipitous encounters in the company.

BUILDING BLOCK 3:

Teamwork & Community

The third block is to multiply advocates and to drop the mindset of the lone expert in companies.

BUILDING BLOCK 4:

Language & Communication

The fourth block requires finding a shared language to communicate within and between every team.

direction the company should go, and what should be done to get there. In terms of research, people have different beliefs about what research is, what methods and processes are best, and who should do research.

All employees—researchers and others—bring with them presuppositions from their previous employment experience and their academic training in their particular discipline or background. Some are presumptions that focus on personal research expertise, individual research skills that translate to what is traditionally valued as "good" research.

In other cases, people begin their career in one role and then transition into research. For example, John began his career as an industrial designer and much of his training was how to make something rather than for whom the product is created. He thus had to shift his mindset and learn a new set of values and beliefs about the role of research in the process.

A common tendency is to only consider research that contributes directly to tangible outcomes as valid. This attitude tends to overlook the value of discovery or strategic research, which is seen as resource-hungry and as having uncertain benefits. As one interviewee, Alice, stated, research success is validated by "getting more money, likes, more engagement": if the outputs aren't measurable, then research doesn't have value. Often quantitative research results are seen to produce these kinds of tangible outcomes, but qualitative research also contributes directly to the development of products and features. This attitude tends to overlook the value of discovery or strategic research, which are seen as resource-hungry and with uncertain benefits. While central to understanding the user, this standpoint creates blocks to communication rather than bridges to the team members.

Another component is questioning beliefs about what research involves and how it should be done. Marian, a seasoned service designer working in a

larger software company, observed that there is a tendency to think of research as an outward exercise and that we forget to do research internally. She taps into internal employees "instead of first going out talking to users." She follows an "Inside-out approach," defined as "look(ing) for sources of information inside...more than not, the problem has already been identified... people have already discussed things...what has happened already" to identify the gaps that she can fill by reaching out and integrating. Therefore, "researching" for her is synonymous with "workshopping" as a way for her to "scale-up" knowledge gathering from 50 people in her unit. As a facilitator, she runs workshops with project managers, designers, and developers to run "research" together and refine, enrich, and uncover information before turning to external users. Other senior practitioners like Kathleen refer to this as a type of anchoring: "You need to anchor the project with stakeholders and socialize it." These interviewees all share a belief that you need to build an "environment of co-creation" for people to talk across silos.

Yet another issue that can arise concerning values and beliefs is how employees view their customers. John found that his colleagues saw their customers as being very different from themselves because they were poor. He told us:

People were talking the language of financial inclusion and financial health, but then I started seeing a lot of "othering" happening: "these people" and almost this kind of fear...because a lot of people in the organisation were kind of used to serving people who were high wealth individuals and did not know about this whole other world that was out there... folks who had to scrape together to get by and were largely working in the cash economy.

The goal is "not just about building a research culture, but a culture of curiosity more broadly— when everybody in your company is curious there is space for exploration and asking interesting questions."

The process of "othering" can also occur among professionals. One of our interviewees told us that sometimes researchers forget to apply relativism to their own practice and may be judgemental of non-researchers. This interviewee recounted that she tended to push her own agenda, especially around the ethics of how customers are treated. She learned that she needed to be more accepting of the attitudes and beliefs of her colleagues, and most importantly, not assume that she was the expert on ethical issues.

The first building block concerns the limiting beliefs that can hinder the creation of a curious workplace. The goal is "not just about building a research culture, but a culture of curiosity more broadly—when everybody in your company is curious there is space for exploration and asking interesting questions," as Corina Enache put it in our interview with her. This is crucial because if an organization is closed to ideas, Gunjan adds, "then you are not going to do research." Curiosity is the springboard to commissioning research and producing insights. She explains that if an organization remains the way it is "because it is more efficient and comfortable" then no new knowledge will be produced and the organization will not grow. Research for her means asking difficult questions.

Building Block 2:
Roles and Relationships

Interpersonal relationships are the cornerstone of any culture. When people share common values and beliefs (Building Block 1) it is far easier to build strong interpersonal relationships (Building Block 2), and to then collaborate effectively (Building Block 3).

For instance, software developer Alice observed how having a good working relationship with her product lead results in a synergy between researcher and product design space. The product lead set the direction of the project and targets for each team member, so their good working relationship meant that Alice could not only meet expectations, but also that she could influence how research shapes projects. This is the synergy that results when interpersonal relationships and roles click.

Issues with interpersonal relationships tend to arise when people do not have clear roles and responsibilities or when there is a lack of trust that prevents people from negotiating. This can particularly be a problem in companies with a competitive culture, where individuals are motivated to seek their own advancement rather than cooperation.
In relation to research specifically, we see issues arise particularly when people try to contribute to a project or task, but their contribution is met with resistance. For example, one of our interviewees told us that he has had conflicts with designers, who at times felt threatened by his suggestions to do research. He explained that they thought he was questioning their competence as designers. But, in his view, he was simply attempting to do his job of applying user insights to product design. This type of confusion stems from the overlap of what "research" is. Anna recalled that "UX and Service Designers were previously in charge of research. When they built up a specialist team of UX Researchers, it took a while to understand how researchers and designers could better collaborate. They did workshops to understand the overlaps in the process and improve the handover between designers and researchers."

A significant portion of successful collaboration involves identifying your own preferences and strengths in the research process so that you can build up teams with distinctive roles and contributions. Anna identified early on in her career that "design" consists of two domains: problems and solutions. The former is where she identifies herself and her work as residing. As she put it, "Researchers shouldn't prototype." She had one

One of the ways to build a research culture is to reorganize the teams not by function but by goal.

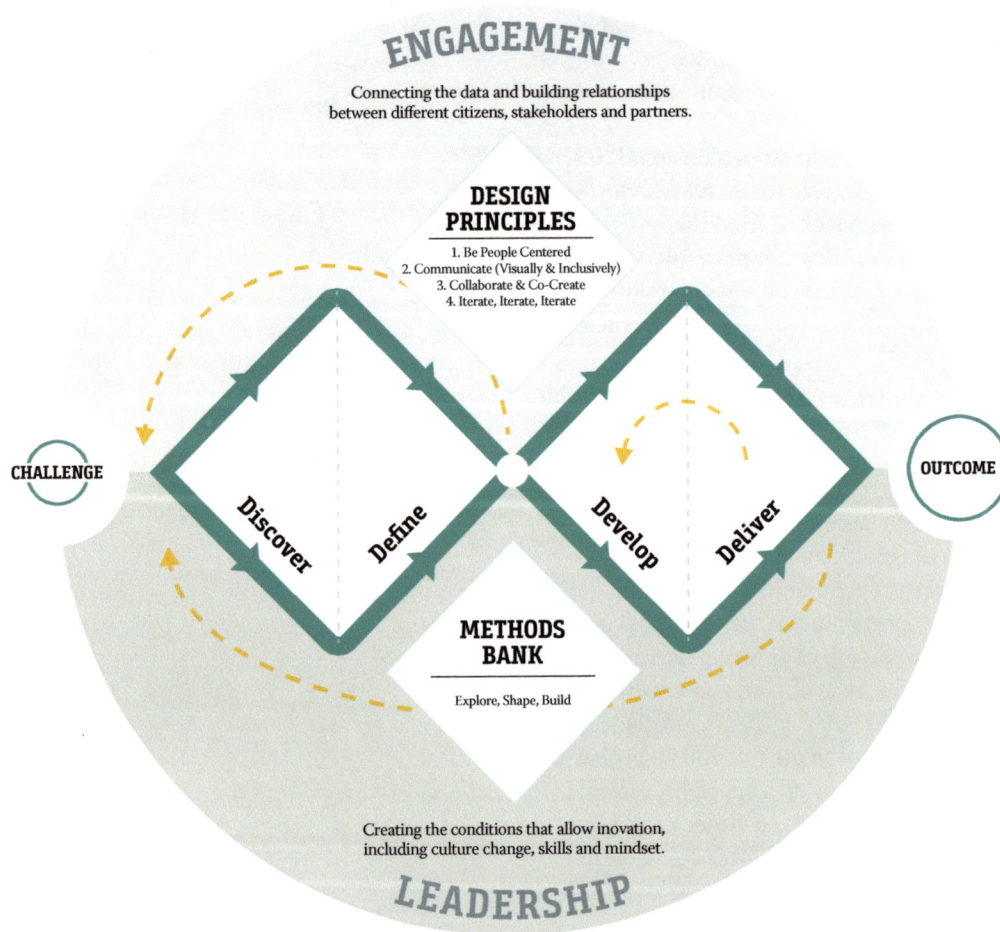

ENGAGEMENT

Connecting the data and building relationships
between different citizens, stakeholders and partners.

DESIGN
PRINCIPLES

1. Be People Centered
2. Communicate (Visually & Inclusively)
3. Collaborate & Co-Create
4. Iterate, Iterate, Iterate

CHALLENGE

Discover   Define   Develop   Deliver

OUTCOME

METHODS
BANK

Explore, Shape, Build

Creating the conditions that allow inovation,
including culture change, skills and mindset.

LEADERSHIP

The double diamond was developed by the British Design Council in 2005 to
communicate the design process to non-designers. They released this updated version
in 2019 to reflect the iterative process of design.

experience where she was asked to create low-fidelity prototypes. She agreed, but found it difficult since she lacked some UI design principles. She felt she was creating more hypotheses at a time when the team needed to be more focused on the solution. Although she agrees that researchers should have an appreciation for business, she feels that she works best in the problem space. Thus, she illustrates her working relationship with her team as having a double diamond approach (see Infographic 4), in which she participates more in the problem space and her teammates, who are UX designers and front-end developers, are highly involved in the solutions space. This system makes their roles clear and relationships smoother.

A similar observation was made by Marian, a service designer, who has to maintain a research partnership with her UX researcher. She agrees that "boundary-making is important in the job to clarify expectations." Importantly, boundaries must reflect the team members' interests. Whether one likes to synthesise or co-create with other members or even do recruitment, it will have a substantial impact on a team's ability to work cohesively. She sometimes finds she needs to clarify her role to non-researchers. She remembered that there was an instance when one of her colleagues thought she was hired to do "detailed user flows and wire flows; that kind of thing where you click on this button, it goes on to this product." She had to tell them that this was not the scope of her role, which led to a clarifying discussion about their roles and the changes they both needed to make to ensure the team was more user-centric.

Strong teams and communities (which we discuss in the following section) benefit from serendipitous interactions outside of job roles and a culture of sharing knowledge and advice. This is particularly the case when conversations expand outside of tactical decision-making or formal processes, and relax into sharing the wealth of experience that colleagues possess. These become opportunities for informal apprenticeship and learning from mentors who are first-generation practitioners in research or design.

This was the case for John, who recalls that, before returning to school to get his Master's in Applied Anthropology, he began exploring a career in user research by joining a pro bono project started by a group of researchers. During the team's monthly lunch meetings he was fortunate to interact with PhD candidates around the kitchen table while eating lunch. He explains:

I was just a designer who showed up and there were a bunch of folks...anthropology PhD candidates... who worked as researchers in the tech industry. And I just started hearing the conversations..about how they were planning out these studies....I was able to slowly immerse myself in the conversations and was invited as an equal to actually talk about things that were interesting, but also realise the complexities of the issues and how much I didn't know about things surrounding inequality and poverty in America.

Having colleagues and mentors who have been in the industry and with more experience helped John to develop:

"a sensitivity... of what the norms were, what sorts of framings were taboo, particularly talking about race and ethnicity, those are the things I was completely clueless on. But also...understanding the tools of the trade, what does a protocol look like... editing those along with experienced researchers, recruiting platforms, often those were borrowed from industry... (like) Craig's List... I had to learn those things even if I wasn't necessarily a part of the first round of research."

Mentors work as both friendly advisors for people who may not even be colleagues, and also as institutional memories for companies without a clear repository. They impact knowledge transfer around not just practical skills training but also discussion around social issues of the business. When individuals take the time to reflect on their interpersonal relationships and to clarify their strengths and complementary roles with one another, then they are well-placed to build strong teams and communities.

Building Block 3:
Teamwork and Community

Strong interpersonal relationships pave the way for strong company communities and great teamwork. As we have seen, good research requires the participation of many people playing different roles, and works best when all players are aligned in the same strategic direction. Following a linear flow of discovery, implementation, and presentation tends to produce a one-way flow of research that leaves little to no room for collaboration with others—team members or the target audience.

"Doing research" should be less about individual expertise, and more about but rather diffusing and multiplying advocates with the research mindset across the organization. In this case, the researcher "self" is no longer an individual but multiple individuals engaged in asking and finding answers.

There are several barriers to building strong communities and teams. One major limitation is the silo mindset in which the term "research" becomes exclusionary rather than inclusive. That is, research as a domain of one specialist versus having non-researchers do research. This applies to the self but especially to others who have assumptions of what research and user research is more specifically.

As we briefly discussed above, Kathleen recalled how, when she began a new job as Research Lead,

"Doing research" should be less about individual expertise, and more about but rather diffusing and multiplying advocates with the research mindset across the organization.

"I told them, no, let's just start with enabling you to do your own research first. And they were like, but that's not in my role description!"

the designers in her new workplace had the idea that "someone else needs to be assigned to our team who will do research, you're here now so you will do research." This specialist approach created a boundary and prevented a strong team formation. Kathleen invested a great deal of time into teaching the designers how to do basic research and to change their mindset that research is only done by specific individuals. She challenged her team: "I told them, no, let's just start with enabling you to do your own research first. And they were like, but that's not in my role description!" She countered with, "Well, actually it is, and if it is not it should be, so let's change it."

Similar to the example of Marian above, but in Kathleen's case team roles needed clarification. Kathleen felt they needed to be expanded rather than contracted. She saw her role as showing people how to do their own research, setting their own objective, choosing appropriate tools, and both asking and answering questions. She felt it was important that she establish a routine in which her team does a round of testing with people participating, taking notes, watching them, and synthesizing together. And the designers learned fast: Kathleen reported that establishing these ways of working took just six months, compared with three years in her former company. This research mindset transformation remains effective even with the remote transition during COVID-19 and the loss of the watercooler meeting.

Sometimes there are clashing definitions and roles within a company such as Gunjan's, an educational institution specializing in curriculum, assessment, and certification. In Gunjan's company the term "research" means developing educational content, building school-university connections, and shaping graduate learning outcomes, not product usability or service design. They also use market research, competition research, and benchmarking, but she says that before she started working there:

"Nobody really went to the users to talk about what is the environment they are living in, what kind of digital platforms they are using right now, how they communicate with other learners"

And so Gunjan began to carry out user research, much to the confusion of the research team, who did not at first understand why she was doing research when they already did it. She had to explain to them how user research is different. Today the need for user research is broadly acknowledged throughout the company—but not without Gunjan needing to lay substantial groundwork. As Gunjan says, "you really have to make some sort of a pitch as to why it answers certain questions or how it's going to benefit."

Alice worked in a start-up environment that hired a user researcher to build research from the ground up, and at first she had no assistance. The user researchers' way of getting started was very informal: she simply gathered people together and said, "let's do some user research!" The user researcher recruited some users for the session and invited colleagues, including Alice, to attend. Alice participated in one of these sessions but did not feel comfortable. Indeed, she felt vulnerable because she is not a user researcher and felt that she and her other non-research colleagues made a lot of mistakes. Nonetheless, the exercise ultimately made them feel empathetic toward their user and what research entails. She recounted that when she saw a real person behind the product they were building, she could feel their pain points, and this gave her the sense that they could fix something.

One of the ways to build a research culture is to reorganize the teams not by function but by goal. This is an experimental approach in which those in leadership and management play between the traditional and more experimental positioning of researchers in the organisational structure.

For companies without user research, the composition of such a team can be more cross-functional and inter-departmental. While this may cause problems with respect to job scope, employees who may be looking for change or switch up benefit from this. The lone UX researcher can usually find personnel who may be similar to her role and recruit them. Kathleen recalled in her previous job, "there was no user research. Just designers. It was pure luck that I managed to hook up with an art director who was willing to do some design work...so that's how we started there."

For companies with user research, the main challenge is where and how to position user researchers in the organization. Cross-functional assignments and pairings can increase research value and impact. Furthermore, this is also an opportunity for non-researchers and researchers to interact and forge greater understanding. This switch-up in positioning is how Kathleen sees how research can garner buy-in the company:

"...a company with different products, different product teams, usually the first thing you do is embed your research in a product team and work on validational work."

To shift researchers in a more impactful role, such as strategic decision-making requires what Kathleen calls"lift yourself up." This is when researchers work across different products, "lifting" research insights up from one product to a company's different products. This may be a panacea to organizations working with traditional managerial structure.

Researchers can help to break down silos, but to do so they need to see themselves less as researchers and more as participants in a process. Building a healthy research culture requires letting go of research control and involving non-researchers in the process. Letting go of the total process control highlights the importance of learning and making mistakes together with the internal stakeholders and team members.

Building Block 4: Language and Communication

As we have discussed, researchers spend a great deal of time evangelizing research within their company, including educating colleagues, finding ways to disseminate their insights, and campaigning for different kinds of research to be done. As Lisa, a digital marketer says, "a big part of my research is communication." Indeed, communication is the bedrock of both research and practices of community building and management.

An important part of this effort is finding a shared language in which to communicate between people from different backgrounds. In most cases, the tangible and intangible products of research become the shared language itself. Design teams, marketing teams, and finance teams may have their own terminology or preferred topics but prefer and understand particular forms of communication: such as data (qual/quant), artifacts (eg, journey maps, customer profiles), or wireframes for product design.

Communication always involves power and politics (and, some would say, power politics). The researchers we spoke with work hard to get a "seat at the table" where they can speak directly with executives about their ideas. This is easier to achieve in startups, where anyone can talk to the CEO directly, as Lisa recounts regarding her previous job in a gaming company. In contrast, it is more difficult to gain this proverbial seat at the table when companies are large and/or hierarchical in structure.

For good teamwork (Building Block 3) to take place, and to produce great products and services (Building Block 7), solid communication (Building Block 4) is absolutely essential. Our interviewees have found many ways to improve communication across teams and their entire company. We describe some of these in the following section.

Techniques to Promote Research

Periodic Sharing of Insights

Kathleen's company sends all employees one insight every week, either user research or quantitative research. She explained, "...It can be no more than 5 or 6 lines, one PDF. Something to keep everyone interested." The goal is to nurture curiosity, but also to "mythbust" what people think users do or to show that they are not using product features in the ways the designers intended. Kathleen reports that the weekly insights have become very popular across the company. By making them explicit, she is both cultivating a culture of curiosity and showing the value of research.

Sometimes weekly insights are more unstructured and serendipitous. This is especially true for those who are lower in the chain of power and authority, such as John, as they must find other ways to influence or anticipate future collaborations. As John put it:

"Standing in that kitchen was the most productive thing we did with our morning, before team meetings just standing there and everyone would be talking loudly about, you know, political trends and demographic shifts. Sometimes people get interested and they get drawn into the conversation and often there are folks from other sides of the organisation, who are much more senior, and it's much harder to have those sorts of informal conversations, especially again for me as a relatively junior person who isn't always in the meetings with them to have some face time."

These types of encounters are what John describes as the meat of what happens outside of meetings because they provide space to converse with people properly and reveal their topical passions. This way they can see him as a person beyond someone doing research, and this "often comes out only in the one on one." However, working from home during COVID-19 restrictions has curtailed these informal chance encounters to build new connections.

Reports

Some researchers find that producing reports for internal use within their company works well as a strategy to get research insights across. For instance, Gunjan told us that the managers in a different office from her now appreciate the user journeys and personas she creates. However, "they're not active champions" of this kind of work, so it is important for her to continue to explain her work through writing reports to share with her colleagues. This then prompts her colleagues to come to her to ask how they can use such research themselves.

However, reports are not necessarily sufficient to communicate successfully across their client's organization. As Anna told us:

"...we never deliver just a research report ever... we look to move forward to implement that research, to work on a strategy...otherwise, the 'research report' we deliver will only stay with the product team, marketing team, who requested it."

Reports may be useful, but they often need to be backed up with a more concrete and tangible output.

Workshops

Workshops are great ways to transfer knowledge and skills, and they need not be overly complex activities. They may involve lone UX researchers bringing together a group of usability testers from different teams or departments.

"Workshopping" is Marian's main tool to scale up knowledge and technical expertise in her software company. She organizes workshops regularly to discuss problems her team is currently working on and uses them to push the work forward. As she explains:

"More often than not, the problem has already been identified. People have already discussed things. I heavily rely on workshops. Like what has happened and what are the gaps that I can fulfill by reaching out."

Workshops benefit Marian by taking digital discussions on platforms like Slack to physical interactions. To a certain extent, reflection occurs on digital platforms when it comes to frameworks and processes, but clarifying issues are best done in person. One time, Marian gave a workshop on service design because the term is so "fuzzy." She explained:

"I gave a presentation called 'What is service design?'—not the theoretical aspect but how to help the unit, like what I want to focus on. I gave that presentation to 50 people and I got questions and it was nice to create a shared understanding."

Another use of workshopping is to hold ideation and gallery style sessions with stakeholders. Anna likes to use these kinds of workshops with external clients. She explains:

"We have such a short time to do research, even if it is foundational, and our clients are dealing with this every day... it is important to have them criticize our findings, help us to analyze it."

Workshops also produce tangible outcomes that contribute to structural or process changes. Alice

Sharing Insights	Workshops	Reports	Metrics	Covert Tactics
· Sharing insights in meetings	· Design sprints	· Research briefs	· Customer participation hours	· Water cooler conversations
· Emailing weekly insights	· Lightening jams	· White papers	· Number of studies done	· Communicating in group activities
· Daily stand-ups	· Event storming	· Topical reports	· Number of usability tests	· Asking senior colleagues to communicate to executives
· Presentations	· Journey mappings	· Educational brochures	· Numerical outcomes	· Adding questions to research that are outside the agreed scope
· Company magazines	· Ideation sessions	· Including journey maps and infographics		
	· Gallery style sessions			

saw one outcome in which a designer-led workshop produced a "committee for design" that adjudicates any conflict or clash in ideas between developers and designers. This workshop-led outcome helped resolve hours of arguments and move products quickly for user testing.

The most important aspect of this exercise is using all available resources to get the research done efficiently and effectively. The more seasoned hands on deck, the more the team can ensure that the results of the research are aligned with the client's needs.

Metrics

Metrics can be an excellent way to communicate research outcomes to a broader audience, especially when management is involved. However, creating relevant metrics for qualitative research can especially be challenging.

Researchers are often highly passionate about their craft and keen to see their insights used to improve the company's products and benefit end users.

Kathleen devised a "research barometer" metric in which her team quantified how many people each product team talked with every week over the course of a year. They tallied the results at the end of the year so they could communicate numerical messages to their colleagues, such as "This year we've talked to 450 of our customers," and show how this was divided up by the different product teams they worked with. Their leadership loved this approach, even though the team were simply presenting a compressed figure of usability testing.

While Kathleen felt that the metrics were essentially meaningless from a research perspective and could be potentially harmful, since they fostered competition between product teams, she believes the exercise was ultimately useful because "it sparked something in people...it does something that I do want to happen... it works for you."

Covert Tactics

When overt communication strategies fail or are not feasible, researchers may use covert methods to get their voices heard. For example, John makes use of what he describes as "the whisper side," trying to indirectly influence those who are in positions of power. He told us:

"When our chief design officer is working with us, we will often feed him sorts of things that we want him to whisper to the executives...he will usually put his own spin on it but he will usually ask us for priorities that we want to have communicated and will figure out ways to get those into the conversation."

Researchers are often highly passionate about their craft and keen to see their insights used to improve the company's products and benefit end users. Thus researchers may spend quite a lot of time doing such politicking to get their messages across, especially when they are either junior employees or when a company's research culture is not strong.

Ways Forward

In this report we have presented some food for thought on how your company can benefit from building a research culture in which all kinds of research and researchers are valued and mobilized to benefit your company and clients. We have focused especially on user research, which we feel is particularly prone to being misunderstood.

We have provided a structure you can build on and some examples of how researchers and their colleagues are currently tackling the problem. In particular we hope that these examples help practitioners improve their working environments and the results of the application of their research.

However, we must emphasise that it takes the efforts of a whole company to move from low research maturity to high research maturity. Research practitioners can do a lot, but their work will always be incremental and partial unless their efforts are integrated into the company's vision and strategy.

In this final section we provide some practical advice for how you can make a research culture into a reality for your organization.

Implementing the Building Blocks

Make curiosity a top-level priority

The most valuable thing you can do to build a healthy research culture in your company is to foster a culture of curiosity. You could say that curiosity is the smallest unit of research: it is the material that makes up the building blocks. Curiosity will motivate people to ask questions, talk with each other, question their own beliefs, question beliefs about customers, and to think about where the company is headed. Without such curiosity you will be hard-pressed to build a research culture.

- How do we break down the barriers that stop people getting curious about things outside their domain?
- How might curiosity help us serve our customers better and improve employee well-being?
- People are curious about different things depending upon their background, such as their job role, personal interests, and so on. How do we stimulate the curiosity of this diverse range of people?
- How might we foster an environment in which people can ask questions?

- Do our hiring practices work against the goal of increasing curiosity?
- How can we hire more curious people? What kinds of profiles might these prospective employees have?

Figure out what role user research should have in your company

User research can play many roles in your company. Do you want user research to contribute to understanding your customers? Designing new products? Improving features? Or even feeding into your company's overall strategy?

In order to identify what role you want user research to play it can be helpful to use workshopping techniques that (as we have seen) are often favored by user researchers. You may like to get together a small mixed team including professionals such as executives, product managers, innovation officers and (of course) "researchers" (designers, analysts, ethnographers, and so on). The big questions to ask are:

- What are my organization's short-term, medium-term, and long-term goals?
- What obstacles and risks stand in the way of meeting these goals?

- What knowledge do we need in order to be prepared? (eg, information about the market, customers, clients, trends, and global events)
- What does 'research' mean to us? (eg, qualitative research, data analytics, operational research, market research)
- What is the potential value of these different kinds of research to our company?
- Operationally, how can we structure communication, teams and workflows to ensure research contributes value to our company?

Audit your research practices

In large organizations research and data collection tend to be done in different departments. Nobody has an overview of all the knowledge being created, and it is rarely brought together. Besides, as we have discussed, people with a formal research role aren't the only ones who collect, analyze, and manage data. You might find that your company has more researchers than you thought. Auditing your current practices will give you a sense of who in your organization is acting as a researcher, even if this is not their job title, and how the data and insights they collect are being used.

Questions to investigate in your audit include the following:

- What data collection and insight generation do we currently do across our entire organization? (e.g. research, marketing, IT, customer service)
- Who produces these data and insights, and how are they used?
- What are these data and insights collected for? Who is the target audience and who are excluded from listening to your results? Can you expand your audience?
- How are these data and insights shared, and with whom?

- How much of it is used, and for what? How much is wasted?
- How is it processed, and how is it stored?
- Which of our performance metrics are vanity and which are impactful ones? How can we redefine our metrics to satisfy both financial and goals?
- What can we do better to share data and insights across the entire company? What barriers are in the way of data sharing? (e.g. technical, differences in employees' skills, confidentiality, regulations, company structure)

Audit your research culture

As a group, companies and teams can set their own detailed criteria and metrics around curiosity, communication, and teamwork that are important in their context. For instance, how are questions and problems asked and answered in the organisation? From here, the building blocks can help prompt further questions.

Questions to ask include the following:

Building Block 1: Values and Beliefs
- Does our organization have a broad culture of curiosity? In what ways or areas might such a culture be lacking?
- What are our company's core beliefs about its purpose, the direction the company should go, and what should be done to get there? To what extent are employees aligned on this?
- What are the prevailing beliefs about what research is, why it is valuable, what methods and processes are best, and who should do research?
- Does our organization have a broad culture of curiosity? In what ways or areas might such a culture be lacking?
- To what extent are values shared across our company, in terms of both company values and the value of research?

Auditing your current practices will give you a sense of who in your organization is acting as a researcher, even if this is not their job title, and how the data and insights they collect are being used.

- What are the limiting beliefs that prevent people from contributing to a project, either because they exclude themselves or exclude others?
- How do our personal backgrounds of employees affect our beliefs and actions within our company?
- What data biases do we currently have in terms of how we collect and interpret data? How can we correct them?
- How do values and beliefs affect how we view our customers?

Building Block 2: Roles and Relationships

- Does the spatial environment of our workplace encourage serendipitous encounters of people across departments? If not, how can we create this?
- Do our job descriptions reflect what we think we are doing or what we should be doing? What might we change? Are there duplications, overlaps or gaps?
- How do personal characteristics, mindsets, and egos affect interpersonal relationships and doing research?
- Does our company have a culture of cooperation or of competition?
- Are we willing to assist and mentor their colleagues?

Building Block 3: Teamwork and Community

- Who is currently leading research in our organization? At what level: team, department, or company?
- Who is doing research? Are they officially researchers or do they have another formal role? How can we help train people who want to move

into this role? How can we scale researcher training in the organisation?
- Are our researchers diverse enough in terms of their backgrounds, levels of experience (juniors are important) and ways of thinking? Or are we hiring more of the same? What hiring regimes empower or disempower people from different backgrounds from joining your teams?
- Are people capacitated to take charge of research (eg, how to do their own research, setting their own objective, choosing appropriate tools, and both asking and answering questions)?
- Are our researchers working in silos, and if so, how can we help them to work together with other members of the organization?
- Are all relevant team members and stakeholders aligned on what the end-goal is and what needs to be done to get there?
- Do our researchers have the opportunity to contribute to strategy? Do they have a "seat at the table"? How is their participation empowered or disempowered?
- What can't we do internally? What do we need to outsource? How do we ask for help?

Building Block 4: Language and Communication

- Do we have a shared language to discuss your work across different roles, teams, and departments?
- What methods and artifacts are used to facilitate communication across roles, teams, and departments?
- What communication issues create confusion or reduce clarity (eg, terminology, the definition of roles or metrics)?

- How do company structure and power politics influence communication?

Make a plan

Write down a plan for developing a research culture that aligns with your goals. Questions you might ask include:

- How can we move from incremental changes to wider, more systemic change?
- How can we move past old behaviors, such as when departments are entrenched or people are used to their old job descriptions and structures?
- How can we engage others to participate in making changes at their level?
- How are we able to evolve job descriptions and tasks that embed curiosity? Not as additional "work" but part of their work?

Rather than a hard plan or roadmap, allow for mistakes and a robust feedback loop to inform next steps and options. Then, implement your plan, experiment with it, and iterate based on the results.

Building a Research Community

Beyond your own company there is a whole community of professionals and organizations that are struggling with similar issues. We encourage you to reach out to them to share your experiences, experiments, and failures. Whatever you are facing, chances are that others have been through it before—and many have blogged and spoken about it (see Learn More). And if you are proud of your research culture, why not share your best practices with the community? Make your company the proof of concept on how to do it right.

Good luck and we hope you have fun building a research culture and a research community!

Learn More

PROFESSIONAL NETWORKS

AIGA
AIGA is the design profession's oldest and largest professional membership organization.

Anthrodesign
Anthrodesign is an online community that has formed to talk about anthropology and design. Ther website gives you several ways to join their discussions.

Applied Anthropology Network (AAN)
The AAN is part of the European Association of Social Anthropology. They run the annual Why the World Needs Anthropology conference, as well as regular events.

EthnoBorrel
EthnoBorrel's aim is to strengthen our professional skills and advance the value of ethnography through our virtual and face-to-face meetups.

Ethnobreakfast
Ethnobreakfast is a practitioners' group for ethnographers in industry, located in the Bay Area, USA.

Ethnography Hangout
This Slack group provides a space for ethnographers to discuss all kinds of topics, from professional interests to how to survive in the workplace.

Ethnographic Praxis in Industry Community (EPIC)
EPIC is a dynamic, diverse global community that advances ethnography in business and organizations. Connect with EPIC through their website.

Industrial Designers Society of America (IDSA)
IDSA promotes the practice of industrial design through education, information, community and advocacy

Interaction Design Foundation (IxDA)
IxDA is an international, member-supported organization dedicated to the discipline of interaction design.

Interbuilding Applied Anthropology
This Meetup aims to bring academic and non-academic sectors together. See their Meetup page.

National Association of Practicing Anthropology (NAPA)
Based in the United States and a section of the American Anthropological Association, NAPA promotes human-centered work applied to practical problems by linking a network of professional anthropologists working across employment sectors.

Service Design Network (SDN)
SDN is a non-profit organisation committed to global growth & innovation within the practice of service design.

User Experience Professionals Association (UXPA)
UXPA supports people who research, design, and evaluate the user experience (UX) of products and services

UX Alliance
UX Alliance is a network of 23 leading independent User Experience (UX) companies.

UX Community of Practice (UX CoP) and Digital.gov
The UX CoP is a group of more than 1,300 federal, state, and local US government employees and contractors who are interested in applying UX methods to create efficient, effective, and useful products and systems.

UX Insights
UX Insights is a conference and a community that connects UX researchers around the globe, offers resources that spark inspiration, and helps develop skills and expertise.

READING & WATCHING

Developing a Culture of Observability (2019, Honeycomb.io)

Anthropologists Wanted: Why Organizations Need Anthropology by Laurens Bakker, Masja Cohen and Walter Faaij (2021, Amsterdam University Press)

Culture Sensitive Design: A Guide to Culture in Practice by Annemiek van Boeijen and Yvo Zijlstra (2020, BIS Publishers)

Building Bridges between Management and the Workforce by Laurea Ciria-Suárez and Robert Andrew Bell (2015 EPIC Proceedings, pp. 254–267)

Rethinking Users: The Design Guide to User Ecosystem Thinking by Benjamin J. Chesluk and Michael Youngblood (2021, BIS Publishers)

Disrupting Workspace: Designing an Office that Inspires Collaboration and Innovation by Ryoko Imai and Masahide Ban (2016 EPIC Proceedings, p. 444–464)

A Mixed Method Approach for Identifying Emerging Fields and Building Collaborative Teams: Leveraging Network Ethnography to Design Experimental Interventions by Therese Kennelly Okraku, Valerio Leone Sciabolazza, Raffaele Vacca and Christopher McCarty (2017 EPIC Proceedings, p.178-196)

(Fr)agile Objects: Thinking Scrum through Post-It Notes by Isabel LaFuente and Wilson Prata (2019 EPIC Proceedings, pp 237–253)

The Missing Tool in the Design Leadership Toolbox: Integrating Conflict Management into Collaborative Design by Susana La Luz-Hawkins (2015 EPIC Proceedings, pp. 132–145)

Ethnographic Tools: From Insight to Intervention by Wafa Said Mosleh (2017 EPIC Proceedings, p.159-176).

Anthro-Vision: A New Way to See in Business and Life by Gillian Tett (2021, Simon and Schuster)

Tutorial: Agile for Researchers by Carrie Yury and Chris Young (2017 EPIC Proceedings)

Acknowledgements

This publication could not have been made possible without the assistance of many people. First we would like to thank our interviewees, some of whom will remain anonymous. We would also like to thank the people who generously reviewed this report or provided comments: Dawn Walter, Jeffrey Greger, Gunjan Singh, Corina Enache, Kenny Baas, Jennifer Collier Jennings, Kathleen Asjes, Dominique Uy, and Karin den Bouwmeester and Gabriela Vargas-Cetina.

Our heartfelt thanks to the American Anthropological Association for supporting this project and publishing the outcome. The Department of Anthropology at the University of Amsterdam has been a generous and supportive sponsor, and we thank them for their enthusiasm in our work.

We also very much appreciate the dedication of our media partners: the National Association for the Practice of Anthropology (NAPA), the Applied Anthropology Network (AAN), The Human Show, Response-Ability Summit and Activ8 Planet.

About the Authors

Dr. Erin B. Taylor has a PhD in Anthropology from the University of Sydney and is the founder of Finthropology, a company specializing in insights into people's financial behaviour. She specializes in how people's financial behaviour is changing along with innovation in financial services, and has carried out ethnographic research in the Caribbean, Africa and Europe. Erin is especially interested in how culture and group belonging influence people's actions and decisions.

Dr. Melanie T. Uy is a lifelong learner and known for unexpected questions. She is a ritual specialist focusing on the practices of social connection and disconnection and its impact on work and workplaces. Her Ph.D. in Social Anthropology at the Vrije Universiteit Amsterdam investigated how social detachment was essential to the work of migration brokers in China. She currently works as a user experience researcher in the Netherlands and previously ran consumer studies for the retail and health care market in the Philippines. You can follow her @anthrobuzz on Medium and Goodreads for her latest ideas in anthropology and technology.

November 2021
ISBN: 978-1-931303-73-6

www.ingramcontent.com/pod-product-compliance
Lightning Source LLC
Chambersburg PA
CBHW060911270326